Suffolk Voices

Edited By Lisa Lowrie

First published in Great Britain in 2017 by:

 Young**Writers**
Est. 1991

Young Writers
Remus House
Coltsfoot Drive
Peterborough
PE2 9BF
Telephone: 01733 890066
Website: www.youngwriters.co.uk

FOREWORD

Welcome to 'Once Upon a Dream – Suffolk Voices'.

For our latest competition for primary school pupils, we were looking for poems inspired by dreams. This could mean the topsy-turvy imaginative world we visit each night, or the aspirations and hopes we have for the future. Some writers also chose to delve into the creepy world of nightmares!

Dreams provide a rich and varied source of inspiration, as is clear from the diverse and entertaining poems we received. It was great to see how the writers had fun with the theme and let their imaginations run riot, as well as getting to grips with poetic forms such as the acrostic. Inside this collection you will find several poems inspired by the book War Boy by Michael Foreman where writers imagined being transported into the World War II childhood of the characters.

Picking a favourite from the anthology was tough so well done to *Oscar Morariu* who is the winning poet. I would also like to congratulate all the young writers featured in these pages, I hope it encourages you to keep following your writing dreams!

Lisa Lowrie

CONTENTS

Brooke Godfrey (8) 105
Amber Allen (9) 106
Sophie Rogers (7) 108
Evie Ager (7) 109
Mia Merchant (8) 110
Hannah Beth Colgan (8) 111
Louise Morgan (8) 112
Freya Lague (7) 113
Katy Scarlet Ruby Green (9) 114
Bradley Griffiths (9) 115
Jessica Staines (8) 116
Jimmy Edgeler (10) 117
Ella Markham (8) 118
Olivia Rivers (10) 119
Ashton Schaerer (9) 120
Layla Scott (7) 121
Esmée Howell (8) 122
Nicholas John Wright (8) 123
Sainte Murray (9) 124
Ronaldo Miranda (8) 125
Tyler Wilding (7) 126
Liam Turner (9) 127
Noah Brodowski (9) 128
Imogen Linda Janice Witham (10) 129
Isabelle Linney (8) 130
Reuben Francksen (7) 131
Sienna Dumitru (10) 132
Luca Colquhoun (10) 133
Lauren Chapman (8) 134
Megan Meadows (9) 135
Lena Dryja (7) 136
Jasmine Appleby (7) 137
Rocco De-Ath (8) 138
Balian Bevan (8) 139
Evan Simpson (8) 140
Jessica Louise Buxton (7) 141
Alyssia Nicole Fryer (7) 142
Connor McKeon (8) 143
Harry Franklin (7) 144
Gabby Green (10) 145
Amy Cobbold (9) & Kerys Cavendish (10) 146
Mia Walsh (8) 147
Georgie Moulton (7) 148

Centre Academy East Anglia, Ipswich

Katie Parfett (13) 149
Beth Matilda Rose Vincent (10) 150

Dennington CEVCP School, Dennington

Oscar Saunders (9) 151
Connie Yorke Brookes (8) 152
Ned Joseph Langley (8) 153
Robbie Warren (8) 154
Abbie Wilson (8) 155
Emily Clark (8) 156
Fred Thomas (7) 157
Isobelle Long (8) 158
Erin O'Keeffe (8) 159
William Maycock (7) 160
Jack Wood (8) 161
Jesse James (8) 162

Include, Lowestoft

Mackenzie Banham (11) 163
Reuben Wade (10) 164
Connor Moore (10) 165
Andreas Grimble 166

Laureate Community Academy, Newmarket

Karmen Domotor (10) 167
Mehrin Ambia (11) 168
Imogen Castang-Wallman (10) 170
Kacey Beau Wing (10) 171

Rattlesden CE Primary Academy, Rattlesden

Georgina Macro (9)	172
Maizie Carter-Ritchie (9)	174
Josephine Bingley (10)	175
Harriet Owen-Stiff (11)	176
Katy Gilbrook (9)	177

St Mary's Roman Catholic Primary School, Lowestoft

Harriet Glennerster (9)	178
Pippah Olivia Beau Harper-Nunney (10)	179
Jessica McDowell (10)	180
Matthew Page (9)	181
Inuka Rose (9)	182

THE POEMS

Well done! Your poem has been chosen as the best in this book.

The Dog Of My Dreams

I dreamt I had a clever dog
That could even read and write
He spoke the English language
With an accent only slight.

I dreamt I had a hairy dog
Coloured brown and white
He ran around the house all day
And slept in the study at night.

I dreamt I had a friendly dog
Who kissed me when I cried
He loved to play with everyone
And wouldn't hurt a fly.

I dreamt I had a cheerful dog,
He always wagged his tail
He was happy playing with us
And made me laugh without fail.

It was the morning of my birthday
When I woke up from my dream
And lying there beside me
Was the puppy I'd foreseen.

Oscar Morariu (10)
Centre Academy East Anglia, Ipswich

A Magical Dream

The air smelt of bubblegum, strawberry and cola,
You could hear the swirling of the white chocolate
pond
Sadly no one there was called Nola
I turned round and saw candyfloss tree leaves!

I went on my tiptoes, through the mint grass,
Staring around, my belly rumbled
Over a bridge I went, not wearing a mask
Then I saw a gingerbread house!

The gumdrop footpath led me over cream
Staring at the Dairy Milk door
I thought this was a dream!
The KitKat roof melted your heart.

Inside I went, what a shock
There were gummy couches and fluffy flooring
As I kept going, I didn't lock!
There were Twizzler beds as well!

As I headed out, it was time to leave,
I said goodbye to the gummy bunnies
I carefully wiped my eyes on my sleeve
Off I went, now, what's for breakfast?

Isabelle Lockwood (10)
Cedars Park Primary School, Stowmarket

The Dream Of War Boy!

I trot up the stairs,
All by myself,
And get my toothbrush off my shelf.
I walk down the corridor,
Over to my room,
But bring the smell of toothpaste from the bathroom.
I get in my pyjamas,
And hug my teddy tight,
I get my book out ready for the night.
My mum brings up a drink,
A glass of milk and I take a sip,
I start to read *War Boy* and set off to sleep as fast as a ship.

I wake up appearing to be in *War Boy*,
I bump my head
On the end of the bed.
A bomb comes through the window
And I leap out of my deep, deep dream
Me and brother Pud work as a team.
Me and Pud get the sand,
And the bomb gets drowned in it,
We run to the Anderson shelter to make sure we're safe.

I was the church on fire
Those poor old firemen in the hot, long flame.
It's good they have a little fame.

Michael takes me down the green,
We play Indians and cowboys,
With plastic things and toys.
There's this little shelter,
A bit dark and cold,
Lots of people stay in there, well that's what I got told.

There's a plane called Doodlebug
The plane had no pilot and was run by an engine,
If the plane crashes, there might be shrapnel
If you heard the awful thing you had to be ready to
escape.
When the noise stopped, you had to run
And it wasn't much fun.

When the war was over,
There was fun and smiles,
Spread everywhere for miles and miles,
There was music and dance,
And I joined in.
I bet the Germans weren't happy about our win.

I woke up dancing,
And realised it was all a dream
Then I went downstairs to see my mum,
And said, 'My dream was really fun!'

Ivy Ruscoe (8)
Cedars Park Primary School, Stowmarket

A Magical Dream

It was a great day in magical land,
All the sweets were looking grand.
The gumdrop footpath bounced you along,
To where you should really belong.

The sweet gingerbread filled the air
It even attracted a hungry bear!
The Dairy Milk door, yummy and scrummy
Enough to fill your little tummy!

The white chocolate lake, smooth and silky,
Running down it was a little milky
The KitKat roof will melt your heart
While going along in your strawberry cart.

A soft gummy bear couch,
Is enough to get rid of a grouch,
The twizzlers bed is soft and comfy,
Even though it's a little lumpy!

The bubblegum scent flies in the air,
It's really good and fair,
I walked around my home,
Now, what do I loan?

The candy end!

Mya Patel (10)
Cedars Park Primary School, Stowmarket

The Dream Of War Boy!

Climbing the stairs one by one,
I bow my weary head,
I brush my teeth in the bathroom
And then I'm off to bed.
I take out my book called *War Boy*,
And read by the bedroom light.
My eyes begin to get heavy,
I drift into the dreamy night.

The bomb came through the window
And Pud is putting out the fire.
I grab the sandbag from the centre.
I look through the window, and the church is on fire.
Mum grabs me from the bed, and I hit my head.
We run outside and I follow Michael to the Anderson
shelter.
We're all finally safe!

We all run out,
And have great fun.
Sometimes we'd play Germans versus Britons,
The fun we'd have.
I like to play cowboys and Indians.
I followed Michael up to his old Anderson shelter
That he said was his hideout.

We could hear the Doodlebugs coming,
We all were very frightened,
But the Doodlebug was coming, coming,
I ran to the Anderson shelter,
Now I knew where it was.
The Doodlebug ran out of fuel
And was going to fall to the ground,
But the ATL girls were there and destroyed the whole
thing right in one hit.
We found out the next day,
That it landed on a farm a mile away.

The war is over.
Some dads come back and some don't.
Everyone is happy and it's father-children time,
We're all flying kites.
We're all watching the bonfires burn out,
It is Guy Fawkes.

As I slowly open my eyes,
I think, *Where am I?* I realise that it was all a dream,
War Boy is left on the page it was as I drifted asleep
last night.

Jasmine Hall (9)
Cedars Park Primary School, Stowmarket

War Boy Dream

Time for bed, I'm told
I struggle up the stairs
The warm bed welcomes me like a friend
I turn the page of my book *War Boy*
I shortly drift into a sleep of dreams
I drift into a dream, a different land.

I end up in a house of a boy called Michael
Who is in my book called *War Boy*
A bomb came through the window
And next to his toy.
I see them charge to the shelter so I follow them
We go underground to our shelter
We can see the church is on fire as we come out
We also see the firemen putting it out.

I follow Michael all day and the next day we go up a
hill
We play with the Green Hill Gang
We fire arrows at the enemy and they fire back.
We play cowboys and Indians
To make trenches, in Britain versus Germany, we use
sand sacks
I like being an Indian
We play football with Italian prisoners.

When the Yanks came we all ran behind their trucks
We saw massive planes fly above us
They belonged to the USA
They brought new planes I didn't know about
Some of them the gang didn't know about.

We saw Doodlebugs come across the channel
I hear a train in the distance with evacuees on
When the engine on the Doodlebug goes we all run.
Some get shot by the gunners though
We all shout when one gets shot down.

The war is over and we celebrate.
We let spare flares off.
There are three bonfires and we burn fake Hitlers
There is loads of dancing
There is loads of noise.
I wake up and realise it was just a dream
I see *War Boy* where it was yesterday
I go downstairs and write it on paper.

Daniel Taylor (8)
Cedars Park Primary School, Stowmarket

The Shipwreck Adventure

As I drift off to sleep,
With my stick in my hand,
I start to feel a dream in my head
As I fall into a field with my friends by my side.

'We need a plan,' I say.
'A plan for war.'
'What war?' ask the rest of the gang of Hill Green
'War on water,' I reply again.

Nervously the next day, me and the rest of the gang
hide behind a tree,
Wimp, behind the hazel,
Squirt, up above me, looking out through the sea.

Creepily, we slide down the sand
Then jumped onto the nearest boat,
But then in a second the sailors were on too,
Then they were arguing over who should drive...

When suddenly we heard,
A sailor shout
'Look over here.'
'Look what I've found.'

The next thing I knew,
Was that we were sitting on the beach,
In a tangled heap,
Getting wet each time the tide came in.

Then suddenly I have an idea,
'Meet me at ten tonight,' I say.
'Why?' they ask with a puzzled look on their faces,
'You'll see,' I say once again.

Now it's ten my friends have arrived,
We're sitting by the candle right outside,
'Now for my idea,' I whisper to them.
They start to run in all different directions.

Wimp to the field,
Squirt to the beach,
And me to my house,
When we came back we built, built, built until we had
our own little boat.

I wake up just the same
With my stick in my hand
I'm ready to jump into my little boat
When I notice it's not there!

Abigail Brett (8)
Cedars Park Primary School, Stowmarket

War Boy Poem (Kids Version)

Getting a glass of milk,
Having a sip,
Walking upstairs one by one,
Brushing my teeth side to side.

Putting on my pjs,
And getting ready for bed,
Getting a book,
Called *War Boy*.

A kid called Michael,
And a kid called Pud
Pud putting out the fire in the neighbourhood.
Five miles away, there was a church on fire.

Running to our shelter,
And making it better,
Our neighbour's house was burning,
And we didn't know what to do.

Picking up the clean bananas,
And there was a big hole in the ground,
I picked up the clean plums
And I didn't pick up the dirty ones.

There was a Doodlebug flying,
The Doodlebug was about to crash
The Doodlebug was really bad,
And I wanted to tell my dad.

The Doodlebug crashed,
And we wanted to see it,
Everyone was screaming,
And the air raid siren started.

The war was over,
And we survived,
The air raid siren stopped automatically,
We were having fun and celebrating.

We were playing cowboys and Indians,
The place was getting rebuilt,
We started to help,
But we were really bored.

I woke up,
I was tired and sleepy
And it was all a dream
And I had another sip of drink.

It was morning
Sunny and hot,
I brushed my teeth side to side
And I walked downstairs one by one.

James Cubbold (8)
Cedars Park Primary School, Stowmarket

My Dream

Me and my friend called Evie,
Wanted to see a unicorn
We went in a castle made of candy
We felt quite nervous
When we got right up to the top
There was a group of unicorns
They were singing in the moonlight
We found a girl called Mia.
Further down in the cell, there was a girl called Matilda
There was a girl called Emyla sitting on the middle
step.
Evie's hair was as blonde as a lion's mane
Emyla's hair was as brown as a horse's body
Mia's hair was as ginger as a kitten
Matilda's hair was crackling in the sun
The oldest unicorn was pink
The younger unicorns were rainbow.
The baby unicorns were orange
Evie's favourite ones were the orange ones
Emyla's best one was the pink
Mine, Mia's and Matilda's cutest one was the rainbow.

Millie Moore (8)
Cedars Park Primary School, Stowmarket

War Boy

Climbing the stairs one by one,
I bow my weary head,
I brush my teeth in the bathroom
And then I'm off to bed
I take out my book called *War Boy*
And read by the bedroom light
My eyes begin to get heavy,
I drift into the dreamy night.

The bomb comes through the window
Pud is getting some sand
Then he goes back to land
I am running to the shelter
And I see the church on fire
But I see something else on fire
It really shocks me a lot
Nearly everything is a big mess.

I can see the Hill Green Gang walking
I can see them playing
I went to help them play the game
They were a little bit good

I found out they were better than me
They got better and better
Until I could not play it
But they could not play it now.

I go pick up some food
I find someone talking to me
They chatter, chatter, chatter, chat
I found a lady
She was so pretty and nice
The food was so nice
I was nice to the other lady.

The celebration started
I was dancing and singing
There were lots of decorations
There was a bonfire
There was music and people
The war was over
There was partying and dancing
It was a lot of fun.

I am waking up
It was just a dream

What was I talking about again?
Don't wanna talk about the dream again
Looking forward to the next dream.

Desiree Mukunyiadze (8)
Cedars Park Primary School, Stowmarket

The Bombs Are Coming

I was in a street and who did I meet?
People screaming because bombs came falling down
People started to frown,
People shouting, 'Get to your shelters now!'

Firemen are coming,
I saw the front line shooting back
Spitfires flew in to help.

The church exploded.
The sky was red and full of smoke
A boy asked me, 'What is your name?'
I said, 'Jacob, Jacob, that's my name.'
He shouted, 'Jacob come to my house.'

A huge bomb went through the house
It started to fall down
A bomb landed right next to me. *Boom!*

But it turns out it was just a dream.
I looked out the window
And saw where I was, there's the glow
In the stream.
Over there is where I exploded
I am in Lowestoft.

Jacob Cole (9)
Cedars Park Primary School, Stowmarket

Never Knowing Who To Trust

When I close my eyes,
And drift off to sleep,
I begin to fall
Very, very deep.

Sitting on wet, soggy grass
'Where am I?' I gasp.
Then I suddenly realise,
I'm with the Hill Green Gang.
We're all playing
And I'm Peter Pan.

Spotting old ladies,
There's Captain Hook!
Playing on the hills,
Like the ship just shook.

But so very suddenly,
To ruin the fun,
A Messerschmitt flies over,
Not knowing what to do
I'd run if I were you.

Down it dropped bombs,
More, more and more
Like a torn, tatty table's dust
You never know who to trust.

As we take a deep breath,
And we make a run for it,
Off to the air raid shelter,
Where is the Messerschmitt?

Nervously we step out of the air raid shelter
I see the damage
It didn't do much,
Apart from the garage.

The Messerschmitt flies over
To the white cliffs of Dover
Smelling the gas
The clouds crying
Fireflies flying.

When I fell on the carpet of grass,
I hit my head as hard as a rock
Hours ticking fast
On the wide town clock.

Feeling dizzy all around,
Hearing sounds round and round,
I suddenly wake up in shock,
Feeling relieved it's just a dream.

Megan Fox (9)
Cedars Park Primary School, Stowmarket

A Lady Bug's Adventure

Listen carefully to hear this dream poem,
But because it's as magical as pure imagination,
In this dream I'm surprisingly a lady bug,
Small, gentle and calm holding a pink mug,
I, lady bug, travel to awesome places,
Which may settle your brain down for a rest.

The first place I set my eyes on was amazing,
With swishy green grass and lovely flowers that were
just lazing,
You hear the grass and flowers in the sun making,
Swish, swosh, swish, swosh, swish, swish, swish, swosh!
Noises that filled my eyes with total calmness.

I was as calm as a fluffy puppy sleeping,
I know you might think I'm crazy,
But this place makes me sleep easier,
There were breezes as cold as the Antarctic,
I don't care as long as I have an imagination.

Olivia Baxter (7)
Cedars Park Primary School, Stowmarket

Untitled

I slip on my pyjamas,
And walk to the bathroom,
I then brush my teeth,
I walk back to my bedroom,
And get out my favourite book,
Called *War Boy*,
I read two pages of *War Boy*
Then I fall asleep.

A bomb came through the window,
It gave me a fright,
Pud put out the fire,
As we ran away
But as we got to the shelter
The church was up in blazes
The firemen were there
Putting out the fire.

All the teachers are kind
But some could be bossy
Our teacher is old
And whacks us with a ruler

And that is what she did
When we did the goose step
In front of her
That was a bad moment.

A Doodlebug is a machine
A robot that goes *bang!*
I watch it soar above me
As I'm wondering where it's going
I follow it to a barn
And then the ATS girls
Shoot it down
To the ground.

The war is over
I sing a little song
I dance a little dance
I am happy as ever
Someone had a hay bale
With some Hitlers on it
Made of straw
And they are set alight.

I wake up with a jolt
And open my blinds

I take off my pyjamas
And put on my clothes
I wonder what Michael is doing
Now and realise
It was just a little dream.

Duke Ecclestone (8)
Cedars Park Primary School, Stowmarket

The Hill Green Gang

As I drift off to sleep,
In my warm cosy bed,
I begin to imagine,
The Hill Green Gang in my head.

I was playing with the Hill Green Gang and Michael
We were a bit bored so we had some fun,
We went to the air raid siren
And we climbed up a ladder,
Then we clicked on the 'on' button
Running to the sweet shop
I grabbed a jar of gobstoppers
And a bar of chocolate,
Wimp just ate horse poo,
Squirt had pear drops,
But they looked just like props,
And Michael had lemon sherbets
We then grabbed all the money from the cash register,
We ran to the air raid siren
And turned it off
But suddenly... *boom!*

I woke up in my bed,
Thinking what was going on in my head,
Then I just went back to sleep.

Jack Brown (8)
Cedars Park Primary School, Stowmarket

Haunted Woods Nightmare Dreams

H aunted houses are nightmares,
A nd nobody else is here.
U nder the branches are twisted trunks,
N ow, with trembling fingers, I carry on.
T wisted iron gates blocking my paths,
E rie shadows looking like wolves,
D arkness haunts you, making you want to turn back.

W ood flaking off branches as slowly as a slug,
O n and on I go, hearing big bangs
O ver and under trees that try to smack me.
D ancing in the moonlight if you would dare,
S unshine in no other place except a lair.

N ightmares haunting me everywhere I go,
I want to turn back but I can't.
G rass walls form from where I've looked behind.
H arder and harder they suck out happiness
T o the point where your soul is lost.
M y heart is beating as fast as a drum
A nd my feet are thudding and pounding.
R ed eyes glinting up and round at me,
E choing in the darkness are my screams.

D im lights illuminate these few things,
R eluctant to where I go.
E mbers aren't shining as dark magic is about.
A ll my hopes are fading away,
M agic doesn't help me get through this.
S hould I stay here? For I know it's just a dream.

Ellie Waldock (8)
Cedars Park Primary School, Stowmarket

My Great Sailing Trip

I went to bed,
I shut my eyes,
All that was in my head
Was the Hill Green Gang.

Suddenly, I was next to the corner shop
I was with Michael and the Hill Green Gang
Then I heard a little bang
It was Michael with an idea.

'What was it?' I asked.
It was to play kick the can,
So we started to play
After a bit we got bored.

Then the Hill Green Gang decided to do something
different,
They decided to go on a sailing trip,
Because the sailors weren't there
So we went on the boat.

After a bit,
I felt the sea
It was like blue hands waving at me,
It made me giggle and smile a lot.

Then I saw a German plane,
Not another one again,
We were all screaming,
We were yelling for help.

All of a sudden,
I saw the sailors,
My eyes lit up,
Just like lanterns.

They had a big boat,
It was blue,
Our boat was small,
So we jumped on theirs.

We managed to escape,
The German plane was gone,
We got back to the corner shop,
Inside the sweet shop, I heard a little pop.

It was Michael with fizzy sweets,
Happily, the sailors winked at me,
It made me giggle,
And smile a bit.

Amy Young (8)
Cedars Park Primary School, Stowmarket

I Had A Dream About War Boy

I am told to go to bed
I jump into my pyjamas
I try not to bang my head.
Brush my teeth until they start to gleam
And grab a book called *War Boy*.
And get a hot chocolate then,
I drift off into the land of dreams.

I see a whirling light,
I open my eyes to see
It is still night
But I'm in house with a bomb.
In this room is a boy.
Another carries sand.
That bomb is not a toy!
We run to a shelter.

The voices in the shop
Begin to get on my nerves
Then all of a sudden, the voices drop,
Soldiers stride in one by one
Then the boy I saw earlier got spotted,
So did a girl with frilly hair,
And a lady whose dress was dotted
So I ran and ran and ran.

I went to have some fun,
So I played capture
Until we were done.
I was a cowboy and they were Indians.
We played until the sun went down.
But then it started to rain.
We went home, each with a frown.
It was so fun.

It was the end of the war,
We danced and sung and pranced.
Bonfires lit with Hitlers on.
We cheered, 'It's over.'
Everyone was happy.

I woke up smiling,
I told my parents all about it, but something wasn't right.

Isabella Cerys North-Fields (8)
Cedars Park Primary School, Stowmarket

The Never Quitters

As I drift off to sleep,
In my warm cosy bed,
I begin to imagine,
The Hill Green Gang in my head.

Me and the Hill Green Gang
Pretend to shoot the gran,
We see our enemies, the Botright brothers
But then we look at the others.

When we said, 'Let's have a football battle.'
The Botright brothers said, 'You won't beat us.'
But we must,
Because we are the never quitters.

The Botright brothers saw me running,
They tripped me up,
And I landed on a soggy cup,
But I get up and say, 'I'm a never quitter.'

So we race on our bikes,
Someone said they liked my bike,
So the Botright brothers got jealous,
So they tripped me up on my bike.

My bike goes flying,
I start sighing
I fly through air and I land on the finish line.

I got up and said, 'I'm just fine but I don't quit.'
We went to the corner shop,
We found a mop,
We got the mop and hit it on the Bot brother's head.

They hit me back,
I get the sack of sweets,
I hit them with it.

I wake up in my warm cosy bed,
I said, 'What a weird dream.'
But it was funny.

Frances Christian (8)
Cedars Park Primary School, Stowmarket

Unicorn Parks

The two girls are falling asleep
And they won't wake up until the alarm goes beep
As the dreams tie together
The dreams they have will stay forever
Soon they bounce on a planet or two
While the cows on Earth go moo
And while they look around they say,
'I hope we don't have to pay to stay!'

Then they spot an old wooden stable
With unicorns sitting at a table!
Soon one comes up and asks,
'Would you like a ride around the parks?'
Of course the girls went, 'Yes please! Yes please!'
But then they worried about paying some fees.
'Don't worry, don't worry!' the unicorn said.
'We're free until we go to bed!'
The girls jumped up on its back,
Afraid the master would give them a whack.

Soon they were back from the parks
They hadn't even got a few marks!

But then it all went quite bad,
The unicorns had gone mighty mad!
'It's time for you to go back,' they cried
'And we really hope you never lied.'
As you can see it really was bad
The unicorns had really gone very mad!

Soon they were back and not asleep,
For the alarm had gone *beep, beep, beep!*

Maisie Perkins (10)
Cedars Park Primary School, Stowmarket

My Dream

I have a glass of milk,
I walk into my bedroom
I put on my thick pyjamas
I start reading War Boy
And toss aside my small toy,
I drop my sleepy head to the pillow.

A bomb comes through the roof,
Mother tells me to get back,
Brother Pud puts some sand on it
We run to the shelter
We run to the big shelter
We run to the shelter really fast.

Cowboys and Indians
That's what Hill Green Gang played
We played English and German too
Mrs West is teaching
Mrs West is teaching us
Mrs West is teaching us very well.

I hear the Doodlebug
The loud Doodlebug I hear

The Doodlebug is about to land
We run to the shelter fast,
So we can survive the Doodlebug
When it lands we go back to school.

Everyone's dancing
Soldiers are dancing happily
Children are joining in the dance
We burned down straw Hitler's
The Americans join in.
Then we head home to live our lives.

'Why was that a dream?' I said,
I got out of my football bed.
Mom said, 'Come for breakfast.'
I said, 'I had a dream,
About war and *War Boy*.'
She said, 'No whipped cream.'

Caleb Marcus Wright (9)
Cedars Park Primary School, Stowmarket

The Sweet Treat

Drifting off to sleep,
In my warm cosy bed,
I begin to imagine,
The Hill Green Gang in my head.

I go to Michael's huge house
And his mum makes us a delicious lunch,
I found it really nice,
Then Michael says, 'Let's play catch.'

So then we go to the hill green,
And we meet our friends Squirt and Wimp,
Then the Botwright brothers come,
That's when we think we have to run.

But they've come to say,
'All we want to do is play.'
So we say OK,
They play with us but they take our sweets.

Then I begin to yell,
But then Michael tells me,
That he hit them on the head,
So we got to try and find them.

Eventually we find them and,
Tell them what happened,
They forgive us and we become friends
Then we start to play catch again.

Then we all go back to Michael's house,
There we meet Squirt and Wimp
Michael's mum makes us tea,
And we have a great time together.

Suddenly I wake up,
I can't believe it's all a dream,
Suddenly I feel really weird,
Then I feel happy and go back to sleep.

Jessica Lambourne (9)
Cedars Park Primary School, Stowmarket

Mysterious Dream Of War Boy

I go upstairs to the bathroom,
And brush my teeth.
Then put on my pyjamas with a flower on them,
And then get my favourite book, *War Boy*,
And read it whilst drinking apple juice,
Then drift off to bed,
And have a dream.

I'm with Michael my best friend
A bomb comes through the window
Michael's brother called Pud puts sand on it
And runs to shelter.
Then the church is on fire,
What shall we do?

We like playing cowboys and Indians,
And we're jolly and happy.
We like to fight but not for real,
We never fight on our road but on fields, yes.

Then we hear a Doodlebug,
And then we run away,
We have to find shelter,
And know everyone is safe,
Well maybe not.

We have a bonfire and we put Guy Fawkes on it,
Did I mention they're of Hitler.
We laugh and sing,
And we dance as well, you can't forget that.

I wake up surprisingly
The book *War Boy* is on my bed.
Then I get out of bed and go downstairs,
And get a drink and some breakfast.
I get out of my pyjamas and get dressed for school,
And of course, I brush my teeth.

Aldona Sylejmani (8)
Cedars Park Primary School, Stowmarket

The Tank Prank

As I get into bed,
I drift to sleep,
Into a bus in my head,
I wait and wait and wait.

Suddenly, out of the city,
Into the country,
Loads of trees all around,
All the apples are crunchy.

Playing football in the fields that are colossal,
Kicking the ball onto a fossil,
Soon I see Mike,
And he brought his bike.

Mike kicked the ball into a bush,
I go to the hedge and push,
Oh no the ball went through,
Could it really be true?

It's the Botwright brothers,
And they started throwing rubbers,
They head towards the tank,
Mike knew it was a prank.

But I didn't and I ran over there,
And Michael ate a pear,
I got into the tank,
Then I realised it was a prank.

Oh no, I'm in a pickle,
Although it did tickle,
Soon I called mother,
And she told off those brothers.

Mike got me out,
And I saw a pig with a great big snout,
We ran away
Past a cat astray.

Planes come to bomb me,
Argh! I was on what I see,
Laying in my bed in my house,
Oh my god, it's a mouse.

Harley Rhodes (8)
Cedars Park Primary School, Stowmarket

War Boy

I trot upstairs slowly,
And slump into my warm bed,
War Boy is in my hands
I flick the pages slowly
And then drift off to sleep.

I'm in the Hill Green gang
Arrows at the enemy,
They attack back at us
We play football with our friends
Prisoners of war join in.

We chase rabbits about
And sometimes shoot them
Brother Pud gives 'em clouts
We sometimes harvest corn
We don't do it with doubt.

We watch for Doodlebugs,
People shoot them overseas
The controllers have mugs
When the engine stops you run
They will fly on their own.

There were lots of people,
They were dancing and playing,
And cheering and shouting.
We were playing a fun game
It was really, really fun.

We were burning Hitler
And dancing round the bonfire
It was really funny
It was full of stuff to do
I had fun with my friends.

I woke up from my bed,
And I opened my dark eyes
I knew it was a dream
I knew it was exciting,
And I knew it wasn't real... Sadly.

Jake Perkins (8)
Cedars Park Primary School, Stowmarket

The Sweetie Trouble

As I slowly fall asleep,
With my furry teddy bear,
I begin to imagine,
I was over there.

Suddenly, I was playing
Kick the can,
We were having fun,
During the sun.

I was in Hill Green Gang,
We all needed a sweet,
The clouds were crying,
As we were having a meet.

I wanted drops of pear,
Please, I need some sweets,
I will share,
Quickly, we went to the shop.

There were none left,
No gobstoppers,
No pear drops,
No lollipops.

The Botwright brothers,
There they were,
I was with the others,
We could see something,
Something in their pocket.

It was gobstoppers,
Get them, get them,
Scrumptious silly sweets,
It was as amazing as victory.

Happily, they ate the sweets,
As we went back home,
Yummy, yummy sweets
Now we were all alone.

It's time to wake up,
I opened my eyes
It was a dream,
There were home-made pies
Next to me.

Jasmine Rhodes (9)
Cedars Park Primary School, Stowmarket

Lost In A Maze

As I turn round,
And round,
Golden leaves fall on the ground.
Children run
Run and run.
Enjoying the bright sun.
Too many winding paths
People so dirty,
They will need lots of baths
Now I start to feel quite dizzy,
Everybody seems to look,
Quite busy.

Help.
Help.
I am so worried
I could just yelp
I am so lost,
I shouldn't have come here,
Now I have to pay the cost.
Down here,
Up there,
Across the stair.

I have looked everywhere
Everyone seems to scatter,
Not one of them asking,
'Whatever's the matter?'
Suddenly,
I feel a pang of guilt,
I am a flower
About to wilt,
I curl up in a ball,
It is so hot
I wish I had a pool.

The moon is out,
I am still here,
So I pout.
Brrrr!
Way too cold,
Now it is dark,
I am not so bold,
Stomp!
Stomp!
Stomp!
Who could it be?
So I listen?
Because I cannot see!

Daisy Grace Everitt (10)
Cedars Park Primary School, Stowmarket

A Dream Of War Boy

Climbing the stairs one by one,
I head into the bathroom,
To get my toothbrush,
And I go to my bedroom,
I get my new book out called War Boy,
And I read it with joy,
And I drift into the dreamy night.

The bomb bounced off the mirror,
And flew over my bed,
The fire gets much bigger,
I wake up and bang my head,
I see Pud putting out the fire,
As the church cools down from water,
I see a lot of barbed wire.

The teacher is really strict,
'Cause she strikes us on the hand,
And I got kicked,
I'm silent as I stand,
I love playing football.

I was standing next to Michael,
As the Doodlebug came in,
The engine was very loud,
As it came closer,
I felt very proud,
Of me not crying.

The war is over,
I can't believe it is,
We are dancing, singing,
It's so much fun.

I wake up,
Was it all a dream?
I went downstairs,
To get my breakfast,
And got changed.

Megan Fynn (9)
Cedars Park Primary School, Stowmarket

The Sweet Fight

I'm at the Hill Green,
With the Hill Green Gang,
And the Botwright brothers
Who are as mean as a grumpy troll.

We are practising using weapons,
While the Botwright brothers
Are looking at our sweets
The bigger Botwright brother.

Wants a go with the weapon
We say no,
Botwright brother wants a fight,
We say no we want to fly a kite.

Let's do it on Green Hill,
The Botwrights are fighting us
Oh no you don't, fire the slingshot and arrows,
Get them.

We are not fighting,
They don't stand one chance,
It's like the blitz called lightning
We beat them.

Now we are eating our sweets,
Where no Botwright brother is,
Now we can play and have fun,
Like jumping, skipping and lots of energy to run.

The clouds are cheering because we won,
The mean old Botwright brothers,
We won, yay!
Everybody goes hooray!

Ryan Bartlett (8)
Cedars Park Primary School, Stowmarket

Chocolate Paradise

I am dreaming about chocolate that's milky
The chocolate that I like is very creamy,
There's lots of chocolate statues which are silky,
Melted chocolate is very steamy,
Oh, chocolate is so sweet,
It is sometimes hard to crunch,
Such a good treat to eat,
It's nice to have a little munch.

In cookies and more,
And chocolate cake,
You will find it in a s'more,
It adds sweetness every time you bake,
A milk chocolate galore
That you should enjoy,
You should have five or more, 'cause they're so good.

I walk to school and spot a monkey,
Then I spot my friends,
They were eating chocolate which was chunky
At school I got some homework,
It was made out of chocolate,
I ate it and smirked,

The next day I swam in a pool,
It was made out of chocolate,
It felt so cool,
It was so nice,
It was like paradise!

Amelie Harvey (10)
Cedars Park Primary School, Stowmarket

A Dream

Climbing the stairs one by one,
I bow my weary head,
I brush my teeth in the bathroom,
And then I'm off to bed
I take out my book called *War Boy*
And read by my bedroom light,
My eyes begin to get heavy,
I drift into the dreamy night.
Pud was putting out the fire,
We all ran to the Anderson shelter
In a hurry looking like we would die.
The firemen were putting out the fire.
When I was with Michael I saw fighting,
I saw real-life bullets, they were big
I saw a Doodlebug, it was massive.
I saw people having a dig.
We started to attack the Doodlebug
With stones, sticks and twigs
It was so big.
We watched it blow stuff up.
There was instruments playing,
And lots of singing followed by
Lots of marching as well.

When I wake up,
I have the book on the same page,
But in the end, I realise it was a dream.

Jack Davies (8)
Cedars Park Primary School, Stowmarket

Mr Criminal Botwrights

I went to bed,
With a warm cosy head,
I heard a bang,
And there was the Hill Green Gang.

Kicking the can we were playing,
Having fun where we're heading,
The Botwrights saw us,
As we got on a bus.

At the corner shop,
Eating the sweets... just can't stop,
In the corner of my eye I saw Botwrights
Fighting about the sweets.

They grabbed a bag each,
While imagining they were on a beach,
They got the sweets, they ate the sweets,
They were stealing the sweets!

'Mum!' I yelled,
'Mum!' I yelled again.
'The Botwrights,
The Botwrights.'

The sweets are really gone,
'Stop, stop, stop!'
'I tell you what
Four free sweets for all of you.'

Finally, I woke up
Next to a cup,
Thought it was real,
But not.

Chloe Grace Sutton (9)
Cedars Park Primary School, Stowmarket

My Dream

Climbing the stairs one by one,
I bow my weary head,
I brushed my teeth in the bathroom
And then I'm off to bed
I took my book War Boy
And read next to the bedroom light
My eyes began to go
Then drift into the dreamy night.

A bomb came through the window, it was terrifying
The noises of the air raid sirens were so annoying,
The bomb was a fire bomb, we got some sand,
That did the trick, wet sand did better.

The Green Hill Gang are the best,
We play Germans and Britons
I normally lose
We play as well Indians and cowboys.

The war is over
The bonfire was burning hot
Everyone was dancing
There were dummies of Hitler on the fire.

I slowly opened my eyes and woke up
And slowly went down the stairs
I told my mum that I had the weirdest dream ever,
Then I had my breakfast.

Callum Maskell (8)
Cedars Park Primary School, Stowmarket

Dream Of War Boy

I'm going up the stairs to bed,
Putting my pyjamas on up in my room,
Then I go into the bathroom
And brush my teeth.

On the way to bed, I get *War Boy*
Then I go to bed
Out my lamp on to read
Then I drift off to sleep.

A bomb comes crashing through
Pud running down the stairs to get sand
I helped Pud putting the fire out
We ran to shelter, I saw the church on fire.

The Hill Green Gang gave up their hill
They dressed up as cowboys and Indians
They locked up the shed,
For good.

I watched the Doodlebug explode
We all watched it dive in
The Doodlebug had no pilot.

All the fathers are coming back
We burned Hitler on hack hay.
All of us had a bonfire.

I woke up.
Then went down for breakfast
I got dressed and brushed my teeth.

Isobel Potts (9)
Cedars Park Primary School, Stowmarket

Two Magical Lands

In the land of the light,
There is never a fight,
Nothing goes to your head,
It lives with your friendship instead,
In the magical land of the light.

In the land of the dark,
The dogs don't bark,
And the plagues come again and again,
Causing the people great pain.
In the frightful land of the dark.

In the land of the light,
It is out of sight,
Of Mars and Venus,
There's nothing between us.
In the wonderful land of the light.

In the land of the dark,
There is always a mark
Where people have slept,
Worrying about their debt
In the second-rate land of the dark.

The lands light and dark
Will always cause you a spark,
Of fear and happiness the same,
The two magical lands of fame.

Scarlett Joanna Fryer (10)
Cedars Park Primary School, Stowmarket

Untitled

My mother bought me,
A milky white fluffy rabbit,
For my birthday present,
It was as cute as a teddy bear,
Her eyes are red like apples,
And her pink ears hang down to the floor,
The same as being sad,
I loved her at first sight
As she shivered in the corner of her bed,
A red little bed for her red little eyes,
To go beddy byes.

I touched her gently,
As I touch as animal's cheek
Soft like cotton and smooth like silk,
As white as snow and milk,
So I named her Milk
We have one problem,
Milk does not know
She is a rabbit.
She thinks she is a person,
No, a princess
And can boss us around

'I'm hungry!'
'Clean my cage!'
'Let me out to dance!'

Kayden Fisher (9)
Cedars Park Primary School, Stowmarket

The Monster And The Tiger

Off on another adventure,
My friend, the monster and me,
Tonight in the deepest jungle,
What will happen this time - let's see!

My monster, he is friendly,
With orange eyes and sharp canine teeth,
He's short and has purple hair,
And black stripes down underneath.

But he's not the only monster in the jungle,
Something stalks through the trees tonight,
The vines and bushes are rustling,
It is a tiger that is causing the fright.

We run away from the tiger,
But get trapped in a dead end,
I wonder if we could convince the beast,
To join and be a friend.

The tiger creeps towards us,
My monster and I start to shake,
The big cat lets out a ferocious roar,
And in my bed I wake.

Emma Chloe Salmon (9)
Cedars Park Primary School, Stowmarket

A Dream Poem

As I drifted to sleep, I found myself in a dark video game,
The grass was as dark as the moonlight sky
The trees stump was as green as a shiny sparkling emerald
The leaves were as crackly as a firework
In the tree, I heard a lovely little bluebird chirping in my ear while I was walking by
The moon was as fluffy as a white rabbit
The stars were as bright as a light bulb.
The next day I saw squirrels peacefully eating their nuts
It made a loud, crunch sound
I heard hedgehogs rustling, in the leaves on the ground
That night I gazed upon a gloomy white moonlight stars,
Some tree stumps were as sparkly blue as a diamond
I saw a lovely sunny caterpillar eating on a leaf
Then I found more spiky, cute and brown hedgehogs eating berries off a berry bush.

Jayden Birkes (8)
Cedars Park Primary School, Stowmarket

My Dreams

All I can see,
Are the things in my dreams,
From dancing green leprechauns,
To rainbows that gleam.
All the things I do,
Are linked to me,
So, read on and you will see.

You're back already
Just to let you know,
It's raining money!
Too much is happening,
Even an eclipse,
With fiery red sparks,
Flying off its lips.

I am so happy
I think I need a nappy
I just got a flying pig
The pig!
The rare pig!
It's starting to dig
I don't know why
I think it might fly!

I could say much more,
But I don't like to bore
This is a sad goodbye
I hoped you like the rhyme,
It was just
A little poem
About my dream life.

Chloe Strachan (10)
Cedars Park Primary School, Stowmarket

My Dream In Reality

Fruit drops, humbugs, pear drops, gobstoppers
Comforts were my favourite and the best
They stained my teeth real bad
Until they were as dark as a cave.

So that was my dream
Short but meaningful
Growing firmly in my head
Once upon a dream.

I spilt my cold drink
I tidied up my mess
I turned myself around
And all my friends were giggling.

So that was my dream
Short but meaningful
Growing firmly in my head
Once upon a dream.

I went back to my humble home
To get some new clothes
Because I had a wet patch
On my shoulder.

So that was my dream
Short but meaningful
Growing firmly in my head
Once upon a dream.

Romilly Cooper (9)
Cedars Park Primary School, Stowmarket

My Dream With War Boy

I get ready for bed
Because I have a sleepy head
I take out my book, *War Boy*
And close my sleepy eye
And drift off into the night.

Then I meet a boy called Michael
He is in a hill green gang
He lets me join and we go to the gang hill.

Find a Doodlebug,
Wait for it to drop
Run away and then run to our shelter
We hear some more
And do it again!

The war is over so we sing a song,
But then hear a clong!
It was Big Ben
Next to a really big hen
Then the party continues.

I woke up from my deep sleep,
Then looked at my clock that made a beep,
I looked at *War Boy*,
I had a lot of joy,
But it was just a dream.

Jake Hancock (8)
Cedars Park Primary School, Stowmarket

Magical Sweets

Khaki legs, sailors's legs, busmen's legs, more
But do you know the worst?
Little old ladies' legs all over the floor.

Liquorice, pear drops, fruit drops, humbugs,
I found myself in a sweet shop
It had yummy goodies for my tummy.

Soldiers and sailors drank the tea,
Found the saucer, cup in my hand,
With a cigar and a piece of cake.

Party hats and a red button on my nose
A scrumptious drink in my hand
It's Michael Foreman's birthday.

The delicious sweets in my pocket
So much money in my wallet
All the types of beautiful candies.

The cupcakes are so scrummy
But it's a little funny
There is a wasp on it.

Aliyah-Maye Wayman
Cedars Park Primary School, Stowmarket

My War Dream

A bomb dropped on my house,
I panicked and ran
It bounced out of my house and made a boom,
Michael ran outside too
I ran so fast I lost a shoe.

Everyone panted and was out of their mind
The farm house exploded
And I was as confused as I can be,
Then I went to check the rusty shed,
The bomb had broken the lead.

Then finally it was over,
And everyone went back to their house,
Me and Michael went back to sleep.
When the air raid siren went off,
Then I covered myself in dirty old cloth.

When I woke up in the morning,
I felt a small relief
No bombs exploding in my room,
I was surprised it was just a dream
I saw the light of sunshine in a beam.

Jayden Patel (8)
Cedars Park Primary School, Stowmarket

Monster Invasion

M y dream is so scary it gives me a fright
O nly I can dream it all through the night
N oisy monster roams through the street
S o I have to run on my own tiny feet
T hrough the city and around the bend
E veryone thinks the monster's not a friend
R unning, running, running without end.

I n the city he roams, attacking loads and loads
N obody knows he can smash roads
V acuum cleaners are no match for him
A s he can smash them then they'll be in the bin
S itting against a tree in more temper than me
I t was so scary, I woke up with glee
O n my bed I rose
N obody knows if it's fake or true.

James Aspinall (8)
Cedars Park Primary School, Stowmarket

Sweet Dream Sweet

Once upon a dream.
It was extreme,
For day and night
For night and day.

I am at a sweet shop
Full of joy
Full of laughter
Full of sweets you can remember.

Wasps, children standing outside,
Looking at all the sweets and pies
Moaning, groaning, dribbling for treats
Meals for grannies, that's a treat
And they're looking down at the delicious treats
And I hear rumbling, grumbling down the street.

Pushing shoving to get a treat
Smelling delicious, smelling fresh
All gone now, time to get some rest.

The shop is dark,
There are no carts parked
Time to wake up, time to wake up
My dream is over, time to wake up.

Grace Calver (8)
Cedars Park Primary School, Stowmarket

Afterlife

When you die,
You will find,
Two paths,
For your guide.
Will it be Heaven?
Will it be Hell?
Who knows,
Where you'll go.

This is Hell,
It's all dark,
It's as dark,
As a cell.
There are devils,
With bright red eyes,
And they glisten,
In Hell's
Fire's light.
You will only go to Hell,
If you don't do well.

Now onto Heaven
Which is much more pleasant,
It had silky blue skies,
Which float above your gentle eyes,

It has flying pugs,
And kittens driving Lamborghinis
And whatever else comes into your brainys.
Heaven is a dream come true,
Whatever you love,
You can do!

Charlotte White (10)
Cedars Park Primary School, Stowmarket

My War Dream

I was in a dream where we were celebrating
Hopefully someone will take a picture
Now the war is over and the parties have begun,
We stand around the bonfire
Watching the Hitler guy burn
The soldiers won't need cover now
The world is about to turn.

After that we had a great feast
And ate five turkeys at least
We took the bones to the fire and made a blaze
Now we could all enjoy our days
Now the families can return,
And the children can properly learn.

One day later, I had a kite
Now we don't need to fight!
My kite got lost high in the sky
I'm so proud that it could fly
Maybe it will come back to me,
Somewhere close by the sea.

Billy Hammond (9)
Cedars Park Primary School, Stowmarket

The Sports Day

'I hate sports day,' Chloe grunted.
'Same,' I answered.
I had brown medium hair and small
Freckles dotted on my pale skin,
Chloe had dark blonde hair and brown
Eyes lined with dark charcoal eyelashes.
This was the moment,
I faced my opponent,
Waiting to race,
Red in the face,
No going back now!
'Do it for Bronte, do it for Bronte!' I muttered
To make me try and feel better,
I ran,
The crowd cheering my name,
'Go Charley, you can do it!'
It was the relay race,
I went at the fastest pace,
Going red in the face,
'I won, I won!' I chanted,
And then I woke up,
It was all a dream!

Charley Grand (10)
Cedars Park Primary School, Stowmarket

My Evacuee Dream

I'm in Lowestoft,
The target is the shoreline
I say to my mum
I'll pack my bag and ted.

My mum said to me,
'You will be evacuated.'
I said, 'No please don't.'

I finished packing
My mum said, 'It's all fine OK
It will be fine now.'
Pud goes somewhere else.

A spare change of clothes
We went to the big station
Carrying my bags
We never came back home again.

I get on the train
As we go faster along
A big adventure
As we got faster and faster.

It was very good
I wish it was good and true
It was all a dream
It started in Lowestoft.

Molly Talbot (9)
Cedars Park Primary School, Stowmarket

The Chocolate Factory

When I shut my eyes and I saw chocolate and sweets.
I could smell a lovely sweet smell
The smell was as sweet as sweets.
I could hear the rushing sound of the chocolate river
The waterfall was trickling
I could also hear pipes sucking up chocolate.
An old man walked towards me
He said, 'What's your name?'
I replied and said, 'Finlay.'
And I asked, 'What's your name?'
'Jelly bean. Could I show you my favourite part?'
'Yes.'
'Follow me, it's the chocolate river.
If you get into the boat then I will get in.'
But he pushed the boat over
I opened my eyes
Luckily it wasn't real.

Finlay Blagg (7)
Cedars Park Primary School, Stowmarket

My Sweet Shop Paradise!

I found myself in a street
Next to a place I loved to meet!
It was a local sweet shop
A heaven that made me stop!
It was bursting with gobstoppers, humbugs, pear drops,
And liquorice comforts and delicious fruit drops.

Me, Michael Foreman and my friends
Burst into the shop, ready to taste treats until the end
Inside was warm and welcoming
With my nose all tingling
And what's more,
They only cost a penny before!
Oh, I would give all the money in my wallet
To have them in my pocket!

But now the dream is over,
I can let my mind wander.
However, I will always remember
The paradise I did encounter!

Christian Baxter (9)
Cedars Park Primary School, Stowmarket

Lego Is Alive

L ego is my thing
E ven though I'm cool
G o Lego go
O h no, your room is full.

C ool Lego
I t is everywhere
T oo much Lego is cool
Y ou need lots of Lego because it is amazing.

I love Lego
N o, the Lego is alive.

M y Lego is amazing
Y ou have powers.

B edroom has lots of amazing Lego in it
E asy Lego you can build
D id you change me to a Lego man?
R eally fast thank you
O h no, you are the police
O h no, I'd better run
M ummy help me!

Charlie Jones (7)
Cedars Park Primary School, Stowmarket

Enchanted Forest

E nchanted forest so beautiful with swaying branches
from the gentle breeze,

N ot many creatures going out shopping to get some
fruit like blueberries

C onkers are falling off trees in their usual brown
colour

H ibernating animals in their cosy homes surrounded
by leaves

A few fairies were fluttering around, they were called
Olivia and Isabella

N one of the fairies were as pretty as Olivia and
Isabella,

T he prettiest ones Isabella and Olivia, well Olivia was
so pretty, she

E ven had pink wings, she also had a purple dress.
Isabella's wears a

D ress and it's green and she blue wings.

Sofia Munteanu (7)

Cedars Park Primary School, Stowmarket

My Dream With Michael

Mother grabbed us from our bed
We woke up with a very confused head
Me and Michael were surprised.

The bombers were shooting at the church
Trying to hit the wooden birch
Now they hit with a massive bang
As the vicar raised his awful fang.

The night sky was filled with lights
Although the bombers didn't start fights
It was Monday before ten
We were surprised seeing loads of men.

Now their planes turned back
Looking like an awful attack
Now it is done
And one man left his gun.

Now I'm awake, all is fine
And the dream is all mine
Once upon a dream.

Frank Wilden (9)
Cedars Park Primary School, Stowmarket

Dream World

Once upon a dream in Dreamland, there were unicorns on rainbows and mine turtles jumping on toadstools
The grass is as green as an emerald and the sky had a smiling sun.
The sun reflects on your heart with imagination flying in the sky.
There are rivers leading to a castle with fierce dragons saving princesses with hard grey walls and delicate doors and windows.

There is candy all around you like gingerbread houses with Smartie tiles and whipped cream to hold everything up
There is a swimming pool made out of hot chocolate and Haribo floats
There's a strawberry pencils slide with mint chocolate, chocolate orange and honeycomb Matchmakers.

Paige Phillips (9)
Cedars Park Primary School, Stowmarket

My Crazy Football Dream

I see famous footballers
I think I could be one of them
I see we are playing at Wembley
I look up at the sky, the puffy clouds
Now I'm filling up our drinks
I can hear *plop, plop!*
Now we're going on the pitch
I think I can run like Usain Bolt.

Kick off
And the pitch is enormous
My team is passing, I get the ball and shoot the ball
It moves quickly and goal!
The referee blows the whistle.

Half-time.
Kick off and they dribble too quick and score
Now penalties! *Ding dong!* We miss, oh no!
But they miss too
Then it's my turn and I score.
We win!

Jack Nunn (8)
Cedars Park Primary School, Stowmarket

A Trip To The Candy Funfair

Candy funfair, so wonderful, magic roller coasters
Something you want to try for sure
The warm wind blows in your face, it is a nice breeze,
I'm standing there with my family, it's magnificent
I can smell something fantastic
There are huge candy trees!
The grass is so crunchy.
I never want to go back. Oh no, no, no!
Be careful, you have to look out for the candy killer
clown!
He is more evil than the Devil
He runs after people at night and scares them away.
So it's never busy
But there are candy stalls all around
You find him stealing
I can smell candy all around.

Isabella Thomas (8)
Cedars Park Primary School, Stowmarket

The Sea's Wish

As I drifted into an imaginative world,
I saw a humongous fish.
Its body was like a giant wading through water,
Other fish drifted by and one was shaped like a dish.
A shiny goldfish performed tricks and looked as if it
was being shot by a mortar going *boom, boom,
Boom!*
The fish's large fins made shockwaves as big as tidal
waves.
The kelp forest swayed like a bush rustling in the
breeze,
As fish did their scheduled routine, clams opened and I
could see a pearl reflecting in the blazing sun
The fish blew bubbles that went pop on the surface of
the water.

Ben Atkins (8)
Cedars Park Primary School, Stowmarket

The Plane

Me, Michael and the Hill Green Gang,
Were playing kick the can,
While Wimp was chasing hoses,
Then we found some money on the floor, enough for
sweets.

Wimp was alright with poo,
As we were walking a Spitfire
I ran to it, everyone followed me, we all squished in,
It took off into midair.

Soon the ride got bumpy, I realised the driver had been
knocked out,
I sat on his lap and drove,
All of a sudden, planes came out of nowhere
I pressed the red button, a plane blew up
As soon as it was over the driver helped me land
I never want to be in the army.

Jayden Christon (8)
Cedars Park Primary School, Stowmarket

Scared Stiff

Quickly, the Hill Green Gang,
Ran to the air raid sirens,
When everyone was in the shelter,
We went for a wander
And we went for a smoke and didn't know what to do.

We went to the shop,
The sweet ship,
Scoffed some of the sweets,
And dropped them in shock,
And wet ourselves.

Wimp was sick,
And ran like hell,
And the Botwright brothers,
Dropped their sweets,
And said,
'A German plane.'
'We didn't set the alarm off, run!'
The German plane fired,
They dived into a tunnel
And were out of breath.

Daniel Brown (9)
Cedars Park Primary School, Stowmarket

Air Raid Sweets

As I drift off to sleep,
In my soft bed,
I begin to imagine the green hill in my head.

All of a sudden,
I'm playing kick the can with my mates,
Wimp who eats horse poo,
And Squirt, he is normal.

But my tummy is starting to rumble,
How can I get a treat?
Maybe by tricking the air raid siren men,
Let's get the plan into action.

So I have tricked the men now,
This is our chance to get the treats,
As quick as a flash we ran to the store,
Got the sweets
And they smelt delicious.

And we got away with it.

Molly (7)
Cedars Park Primary School, Stowmarket

Seeker Of Treasure

As I opened my eyes I found myself in a blazing-hot
temple,
The city was as hot as a forge,
The ring snake was increasing the heat of the
scorching temple
The walls move and the temple shifts to stop
trespassers from seeking ancient treasure,
The icy sky heats the temple to its tip,
The snakes swarm the ground,
The blaze was as sizzling as a beaten-up pile of lava,
The king serpent was like a giant staff blocking your
way,
Splatter! I hear poison dripping from my fate,
I shouldn't have come to this particular date,
Because now it leads me to total death.

Zetong Sun (7)
Cedars Park Primary School, Stowmarket

Once Upon A Dream

I was in my mum's front room.
Where there is a place to play
There are lots of people in the room.

I heard a noise, there was a bang!
Then there was a person who came with a clatter.
There was a smell of food
It was mum in the kitchen.

Me and my friend Jonny were playing cards with my mum.
My friend Jonny was having a laugh,
At my mum and we partied until midnight.

It was midnight when I went to bed!
The soldiers and sailors kissed me goodnight.
They were wishing that was their little boy they just kissed goodnight.

Amelia Jolly (9)
Cedars Park Primary School, Stowmarket

Sleepover

The girls were having a sleepover,
And they had the same dream,
In the morning they woke up with a gleam...
They found themselves in a mysterious forest
With purple, pink and blue leaves on the trees,
Then they bumped into a unicorn
That had a cutie mark that looked like popcorn,
They looked around but couldn't see anything
When suddenly, Little Mix appeared
And sticks were broken while they dance,
They wanted to go on the unicorn,
So Little Mix with sticks in their hair
The unicorn who had a cutie mark like popcorn
And the girls flew into space!

Lena Idziniak (9)
Cedars Park Primary School, Stowmarket

A Dream Poem

As I fell asleep, I drifted,
Into a fun, amazing dream.
It had a big rain cloud,
And a sunny cloud each side of the land.
On the good amazing side were baby and mummy
bananas
You could also see daycare, shops and the most
exciting thing of all,
The trees were made of gummy.
If you ate it all you could plant another grass seed.
The trees were as yummy as gummy bears from a
shop.
All of the people were bananas
And on the bad side,
Lived an old mouldy banana,
Who lived in the building of doom,
And if you went near his side he would eat you.

Brooke Godfrey (8)
Cedars Park Primary School, Stowmarket

Pug's Unicorn Poop

'Noooooo!'
Down I go,
Down Puggy's throat
Out his butt
And
Wow!
'I'm a rainbow, now I'm floating.'
Along the rocky path.
Through the park gate,
Up the ladder,
Down the slide.

After a while,
He heads home,
That means the bin,
And falls asleep,
As soon as he finishes his twelve hour nap,
He starts,
To disappear,
Five,
Four,
Three,
Two,
One,

Now,
He's gone.

'Oh.'
Oh wait,
This was all
A dream...

Amber Allen (9)
Cedars Park Primary School, Stowmarket

My Mermaid Poem

One day, I was at the beach, playing on the sand
When I suddenly felt all tingly
I had become a mermaid!
I said to myself, *Look at me*
I looked around and there was lots of coral to see,
I swam around and this world looked so cool,
It felt like a giant swimming pool!
I soon met another mermaid and her name was Molly
And she seemed to be very, very jolly.
She took me to the mermaid palace,
And I met the merqueen, her name was Alice.
Then I shouted, 'Oh no!'
Because it was time to go,
But I said I'd be back there soon.

Sophie Rogers (7)
Cedars Park Primary School, Stowmarket

My Life In America

When I opened my eyes,
The hot summer sun was shining down on me
I had arrived in America!
I saw the Statue of Liberty
Which was as green as freshly mowed grass
I saw the glistening lake and the bushy trees in Central
Park
I was so happy, excited and thrilled to be here.
It was like I had won the lottery
Vroom! Went the big yellow taxis down the street
The hot dogs were sizzling on the grill by the hot dog
seller
The red, white and blue of the American flag fluttered
in the wind
I couldn't wait to explore this amazing place.

Evie Ager (7)
Cedars Park Primary School, Stowmarket

A Great Dream Poem!

As I close my eyes I slowly walk out
The wet grass is green as a leaf
And as I look up at the pitch-black dark sky, there is a
golden, silvery shiny star
Swaying slowly across the dark, gloomy sky
And the roses are bright as a golden shooting star
The water is warm as a hot bubbly bath
The warm, nice, beautiful and reflecting water,
The sparkly, glimmering and shiny castle is as big as a
fat elephant
The shooting star went quick as a flash
The leaves were rushing away slowly
And I could hear the music and the music was
delightful to hear.

Mia Merchant (8)
Cedars Park Primary School, Stowmarket

Little Star

Little, little, little star in the sky
Don't go away, stay where you are
Please stay, we can have fun
Jolly little star, please come out
Yes, we are friends now
Little star, what is your name?
Come on, tell me and we can play a game
Her name was Molly
She's really jolly
Little, little, little star
I wish for a jar
Molly, I think it's time for you to go
So this jar we can put letters in
And we won't lose touch
Little, little, little star
I'll miss you wherever you are
Bye-bye little star.

Hannah Beth Colgan (8)
Cedars Park Primary School, Stowmarket

War Boy Dream

Climbing the stairs one by one,
I bow my weary head.
I brush my teeth in the bathroom,
And then I'm off to bed.
I take out my book called War Boy,
And read by the bedroom light,
My eyes begin to get heavy
I drift into the dreamy night.

Aunt Louie was singing and dancing along,
While the celebration had started
There was a big bonfire
We all danced around the bonfire.
I woke up and realised that it was all just a dream
And I saw my copy of *War Boy* and I was in bed.

Louise Morgan (8)
Cedars Park Primary School, Stowmarket

Candy Animal Land

As I close my tired sleepy eyes I drift,
Asleep into my imaginative dream...
The cute bunnies are as cute as gummy bears
Jumping into my slobbery mouth
Everywhere I look there are candy animals
Spreading around me,
The animals are as adorable as blooming flowers,
A candy cane cat leaps into my warm lap
With a gumdrop dog beside me
A cupcake guinea pig lays calmly beside me
Also a chocolate unicorn's flying above my head
The river is as splashy and sploshy as the light blue sky.

Freya Lague (7)
Cedars Park Primary School, Stowmarket

My Dream With Michael Foreman

I was dreaming where I was in a shop
Drinking tea and we swapped our cigarette cards
Some fell out of our pockets
The bombs come down and bombed the shop.

We try to find our cigarette cards
We can't find them so we ask the guards
They don't know
What are we going to do?

When I'm in the shop
I can smell the sweets, but sometimes
They're not ready to sell
All the children have their noses against the glass
Looking at the sweets.

Katy Scarlet Ruby Green (9)
Cedars Park Primary School, Stowmarket

Two Magical Lands

I will tell you about two magical lands
Starting with the light
Where people never fight
Butterflies flying, unicorn buying cheap food for
everyone
My house is made of candy, whipped cream and
gingerbread too,
My mud is made of chocolate and my grass is made of
jellies
And the topping is Ben & Jerry's.

Now I will tell you about the dark land,
But people from the light land are banned,
Creepy crawlies sneak in your bed
And they take the mighty bed.

Bradley Griffiths (9)
Cedars Park Primary School, Stowmarket

In Sweet Land

In Sweet Land, it is as beautiful as a rainbow.
It sparkles like a diamond
The sweet sea crackles when it moves.
Also you can eat as many sweets as you want in Sweet Land.
There's multicoloured sweets
There are all kinds of sweets
It's as lovely as Dream Land
The sweets rush up together and it sound like *crack, boom, bang, crack!*
In Sweet Land, it's lovely and pretty as a rule
Sweet Land is the best thing in the world.

Jessica Staines (8)
Cedars Park Primary School, Stowmarket

Chilli Con Carne

C hilli is yummy,
H ow it feels in your tummy,
I nside it feels hot
L ike a boiling pot.
L ooks like a birds nest
I t is the best.

C hilli is my favourite
O n a cold day
N ever mind being called away from my play.

C omes in different heats,
A nd I like it hot
R emember...
N o red chillis
E specially in my pot!

Jimmy Edgeler (10)
Cedars Park Primary School, Stowmarket

Dream Poem

As I close my tired eyes,
I gently and gracefully float away into my relaxing
dream,
I swiftly land in Guinea Pig Land.
There were as many guinea pigs as you could ever
imagine,
Squeaking happily when they sleep,
Two adorable guinea pigs lay next to me, lovingly.
I can see so many guinea pigs,
You won't believe your eyes.
Guinea Pig Land is exploding with lovely-coloured
guinea pigs
White ones, grey ones, black ones and brown ones.

Ella Markham (8)
Cedars Park Primary School, Stowmarket

The Nebula Dream!

The nebula shone bright high in the sky.
In the centre of space and shone so brightly,
It could blind your face, and so you could
See a million colours curving here and there.

As the nebula drifted far into space
Hoping that one day it would become the brightest
star you and I have ever seen.
The colours changing here and there
Curving like a worm stuck in an apple
Or the sea, dangerous and mysterious.

Olivia Rivers (10)
Cedars Park Primary School, Stowmarket

Dream Land

In Dream Land the sky is purply blue,
There's loads of sweets and chocolate too
The floor is as green as an emerald,
There are no laws so you might get fooled.

There are miniature people in Dream Land,
And they all have the same hair as me,
It's funny because they all drink gallons of tea,
You wouldn't believe me without being seen,
But then, I woke up and realised it was all a dream.

Ashton Schaerer (9)
Cedars Park Primary School, Stowmarket

Candy World

The candy is as colourful as the rainbow
I am with my friends
It is a fun, wonderful, exciting world
Everything is made out of candy.
I love Candy World because you can eat everything
The candy is cracking down when you walk on the
street
You have to be steady walking because the paths are
made out of candy.
The walls will crash down on you so be careful
If you hear a crash, you know something's coming.

Layla Scott (7)
Cedars Park Primary School, Stowmarket

Rainforest

I look around
I see green leaves shaking in the wind
I hear the rushing waterfall
I feel the bumps of the palm tree
Ding, dong! Ten ballet dancers dance around me,.
Their dresses are as soft as silk
Three fairies land on my shoulder
I can smell the scent of the rainforest
I am happy, amazed, surprised and astonished.
I had an adventure!
Then I open my eyes and I'm back in bed.

Esmée Howell (8)
Cedars Park Primary School, Stowmarket

My Great Adventure

I was in a gladiator stadium
And I met someone called William
Also there was a giant amphibian.

It was very bare, I was the only one there
Someone shouted out, 'Share.'

Then people started coming in
After the fight I went home
Kaboo! Kabar!
I was back in my house
'Home sweet home
As sweet as a land of sweets.'
Phew!

Nicholas John Wright (8)
Cedars Park Primary School, Stowmarket

Match Of The Day

Numb fingers tying laces,
My football boots take me places.
Socks up high, don't know why
I'm sitting next to my friend Kai
Baggy shorts in red and white,
Help me kick this ball to tremendous height,
Proudly wearing shirt twenty three,
I'll tuck it in or it will cover my knee,
We walk down the tunnel complete as a team
The opposing side don't look so keen.

Sainte Murray (9)
Cedars Park Primary School, Stowmarket

The World Of Minecraft

As I entered the mysterious land,
It was strange, lots of dirt and buildings.
I entered where it was found
Although there was lots of smuggling.
A villager gave me a house but that was the trouble
There was a very mean mouse called Stuble.

He made a loud squeak,
It was even louder than a leak,
He started to chomp and pull,
He even acted more mad than a bull!

Ronaldo Miranda (8)
Cedars Park Primary School, Stowmarket

The Death Dinosaur Dream

As I was walking in the amazing street of England
I turned around as quick as a flash
I saw a massive and totally creepy dinosaur
'Argh!' I screamed so loud that the whole world heard it
It's a dinosaur and it wanted to eat me!
I said in fear, I had to run as fast as I could
Because it was looking in every single piece of the world to find me.

Tyler Wilding (7)
Cedars Park Primary School, Stowmarket

The Hill Green Gang

I'm with my friends,
Playing football in the sun,
Then we think that we can turn the siren on,
So we can get all of the sweets.

But a German plane flies over,
And sees us,
So we run as fast as a cheetah,
And when we get back everyone is angry
So they think that the Germans are gone,
But it was the whole town that was destroyed.

Liam Turner (9)
Cedars Park Primary School, Stowmarket

Chocolate

C reamy, yummy, chocolate delight
H appy to eat them
O pening the wrappers quickly as I can
C erys pinching all my favourites
O n a mission to eat them all
L ove the taste of every one I get
A lways sad when they're all gone
T ip the wrappers in the bin
E very time I wish there were more.

Noah Brodowski (9)
Cedars Park Primary School, Stowmarket

Upside Down World

In upside down world, the sky is under your feet,
The view from your eyes is emerald-green
Green grass and cocoa bean trees,
The birds fly at your feet while dogs leap over your
heads,
In autumn the beautiful colours shine from up above
The sky under my feet is sunny and cloudy
It feels nice on my feet,
The clouds are as fluffy as cotton candy.

Imogen Linda Janice Witham (10)
Cedars Park Primary School, Stowmarket

Wish And Magic Land

W ith each eye
I fall to
S leep to
H ave a dream.

M agical this is
A nd it says to wish
G ratefully I wish
I ce cream appeared
C alling for more.

L ovely land is here
A nd there is
N o sadness
D o come to this land.

Isabelle Linney (8)
Cedars Park Primary School, Stowmarket

My Dream At War

I can hear the guns banging
The army are as fierce as a tank
The wind is blowing in my face
I can eat the pigs for bacon and pork
I will fight for Britain.

I can hear the bombs going off
I can hear the guns banging
I can see the knives for the guns
I will fight the baddy
There are guns waiting to be shot.

Reuben Francksen (7)
Cedars Park Primary School, Stowmarket

It's Upside Down In Dream Land

The sky is as green as an emerald and,
The floor is covered in clouds,
Birds cheep at our feet,
Plants swipe across my face
The trees are poking me with their branches,
In autumn the leaves change colour and fall from the sky,
Airplanes fly under us, rain squirts us from the ground
The best thing is it's upside down.

Sienna Dumitru (10)
Cedars Park Primary School, Stowmarket

Snowfall

Late December,
In early dusk,
The morning snow saw a walrus' tusk.
As the snow fell the clouds swelled
And the snow's consistency held.

Gentle snow pricked the air
The snow got heavier and heavier with no care.
Crashing and crashing a blizzard started
Causing mega damage for all of the land.

Luca Colquhoun (10)
Cedars Park Primary School, Stowmarket

A Dream Poem

I say *shhhh* as I excitedly dream of a
Beautiful bale of golden hay
Slowly floating away,
In the light blue sky.
My, oh my,
How does it manage to fly?
As high as the sun,
Having lots of fun.
With everyone,
Including a newborn.
Pretty unicorn,
With a glittery horn.

Lauren Chapman (8)
Cedars Park Primary School, Stowmarket

Midnight

M y worst nightmare might come true,

I don't know what would you do.

D on't look back,

N or forward.

I hate the colour black.

G hostly noises give me a fright,

H elp, I scream out in the night,

'T il the break of morning light.

Megan Meadows (9)
Cedars Park Primary School, Stowmarket

The Rainforest

It's as quiet as a mountain that's sad
It's as magical as a fairyland
It's as shiny as gold
It's as peaceful as a bird
There's a drip from the water
There's a whoosh sound from the flowing wind
The birds chirp quietly
There's a slurp sound from my water bottle.

Lena Dryja (7)
Cedars Park Primary School, Stowmarket

Nightmare

N ight is scary

I t frightens me

'G ood,' said a clown

H eavy storms are coming

T o my hideout

M um, it is a clown

A clown, a clown, a scary one

'R un!' said the clown, 'I am going to get you!'

E ye of fire.

Jasmine Appleby (7)

Cedars Park Primary School, Stowmarket

There's A Werewolf At My House

From a warm room, I saw a dark and creepy shadow
It moved as fast as a cheetah!
Roar! The shadow moved faster, *scratch!*
A claw mark appeared on the window
The claw mark was gigantic
It was as big as Tarzan's hair
Is that? Oh my gosh, it's a werewolf.

Rocco De-Ath (8)
Cedars Park Primary School, Stowmarket

Nothing

N othing there is that I can see
O nly the little bench just for me
T he whiteness is spreading round
H ear that tapping sound
I loved the bench that was
N o better than me, it went *tap!*
G reat, now it was as red as a laser beam.

Balian Bevan (8)

Cedars Park Primary School, Stowmarket

Me As Spider-Man In My Dream

I am as strong as a man
And I am Spider-Man
I'll get help from Iron Man
And my webs go *thwip!*
Bang! From the explosions,
The fire is as light as a torch
And we are saving the world
And we are fighting vulture
But the buildings get in our way.

Evan Simpson (8)
Cedars Park Primary School, Stowmarket

Untitled

I dream of a unicorn eating a bale of hay,
The sky was as sparkly as a shining star,
It was as big as the world,
The moon was as bright as the sun
The curtain was as dark as the glimmering sky,
The curtain was as long as the world,
The world was as wide as the sun.

Jessica Louise Buxton (7)
Cedars Park Primary School, Stowmarket

Fairies

F lying through the windy sky,
A ir rushes through your hair,
I saw fairies riding unicorns,
R ushing past candyfloss clouds
I mages rush and blur,
E verything is bright and green
S omewhere you will long to be.

Alyssia Nicole Fryer (7)
Cedars Park Primary School, Stowmarket

The Land Of Lightning

No one knows except me
I am in a nightmare, it cannot be!
I turn to see lightning everywhere
And it formed into a creature, half hyena, half bear.
It started to chase my family
The creature growled and chuckled
But it disappeared, finally!

Connor McKeon (8)
Cedars Park Primary School, Stowmarket

Portal

I drifted to sleep,
I found myself,
In my company
All was calm,
And I can see your face,
We go outside
A portal knocks me out
I get back up
'Cause this is my dream
Don't wake me now.

Harry Franklin (7)
Cedars Park Primary School, Stowmarket

Roses

Soft, gentle
And the sweetest touch
But be careful of the thorns
They might give you an ouch
And it will hurt until dawn
The subtle smell is a perfume scent
Petals can leave a trace of where you went.

Gabby Green (10)
Cedars Park Primary School, Stowmarket

Dancing Unicorns

Pink fluffy unicorns dancing on rainbows
They never sleep and they always keep
Blue fluffy unicorns' secrets
They are very kind and they don't mind blue fluffy
unicorns
Dancing on their rainbows!

Amy Cobbold (9) & Kerys Cavendish (10)
Cedars Park Primary School, Stowmarket

My Dream

Me and my unicorn as sparkly
As glitter.
We are going to space
The twinkling stars and
The moon shining,
Our rocket zooming
In the sky.
We see floating candy
In the sky.

Mia Walsh (8)
Cedars Park Primary School, Stowmarket

The Worst Nightmare

As I drifted off to sleep,
I found myself holding a white mane.

I was galloping as fast as a snake at top speed.

The fire was as hot as the blazing sun.

Georgie Moulton (7)
Cedars Park Primary School, Stowmarket

Dreamer

My dreams are my thoughts that I can't control
I hear the demons of the night and all the scared souls
Running as fast as I can even when I know
There's nowhere to go.

My dreams are also my happy place
Where sometimes I hope I do not wake.

Katie Parfett (13)
Centre Academy East Anglia, Ipswich

The Snow

The snow is soft
It crunches when you stand on it
The whole world looks white
You can play with it
It feels soft and hard
When it goes it is sad
But you will get it next year.

Beth Matilda Rose Vincent (10)
Centre Academy East Anglia, Ipswich

My Candy Castle

My candy castle is made of chocolate bricks and big
and red candy sticks.
It's as big as an elephant
It shimmers in the sunlight just waiting to be eaten.
Whoosh! went the fairy.
Its lake is made of caramel, its roof is made of fudge,
When you step on the chocolate path all it does is turn
to smudge.
The marshmallows swim through the hot chocolate.
It had a marshmallow trampoline
If you jump up so high you can catch a glimpse of pie.
The chocolate is as thick as a brick
Splash! went the pie tumbling into the caramel.

Oscar Saunders (9)
Dennington CEVCP School, Dennington

The Sweet Fairy

She's as pretty as flowers and as sweet as sugar
She lives in a castle made of candy cane with cotton candy towers and flowers made of sugar paper in the garden
Her wings are a glamorous blue like diamonds
Trails of flowers appear wherever she goes
She has a throne of rocky road and gummy bear guards
The candyfloss trees dance in the breeze of her wings
Flutter, flutter and up she goes into the sky.

Connie Yorke Brookes (8)
Dennington CEVCP School, Dennington

King Greedy Guts

The spider's fangs as big as trucks
Eats people, what a greedy guts.
His toxic fangs dripping like water drops
Splat, splash, splat!

Its spiky hairs dancing in the air.
Jumping up and down in a frown.
Eats the king to get his crown,
'Now I'm King Greedy Guts! Ha ha ha ha!'

Ned Joseph Langley (8)
Dennington CEVCP School, Dennington

Stampylongnose

One morning in Stampy Lovely World, Stampy was happy.
He built his house out of strong birch wood,
It was as tall as a school and as strong as diamonds
Torches shone from the windows
Inside was a hot, steamy lava room and a cold water room.
He was happy when his friends Lee Bear and iBallisticSquid came to stay.

Robbie Warren (8)
Dennington CEVCP School, Dennington

My Candy House

My candy house is as squishy as can be.
This grand house for my brother and me.
The gummy bear guards wink secretly as people walk by.
'I wish that house was mine,' they say in a sigh.
Pop! goes the candyfloss in a sudden fright.
'Now it's in my tummy, now it's out of sight.'

Abbie Wilson (8)
Dennington CEVCP School, Dennington

The Beautiful Mermaid

The beautiful mermaid swam into the sparkly sea
Her hair waved into the shiny water
Her tail is as slimy as a fish.
The water fizzed into the moon pool.
The mermaid was as shiny as a dolphin.
Her tail splashed in the blue water.
She whizzes in the wet water.
The ocean fizzed up whilst she zoomed.

Emily Clark (8)
Dennington CEVCP School, Dennington

The Pumpkin

The pumpkin in the corner of my garden all gloomy and scary.
The pumpkin at the bottom of my garden all rotten, stinky and weird.
The pumpkin at the bottom of my garden as big as a tank!
The pumpkin at the bottom of my garden.
My pumpkin turns alive every night and crunches others and turns them mouldy.

Fred Thomas (7)
Dennington CEVCP School, Dennington

The Candy Fairy

A beautiful princess fairy zipped around the candy castle.
She passed the icing sands of the beach.
The tropical rainforest looked so magical.
She heard the shouts from evil rats.
She whizzed past the chocolate waterfall.
She came crashing down and drank from the fresh water.

Isobelle Long (8)
Dennington CEVCP School, Dennington

The Furry Cake

A cake was furry, no way.
I make a cake for Fluffy.
I don't know where he is.
I'm sure he is around here somewhere?
My cat is really fluffy like this cake,
I will just take a little bite, *miaow!*
There he is!

Erin O'Keeffe (8)
Dennington CEVCP School, Dennington

The Smasher

The smasher was strong and deadly
He was as tall as a T-rex.
He was as fierce as a sabretooth tiger
He could smash buildings with one tap
With two taps he could smash hotels
With three taps he could smash skyscrapers.

William Maycock (7)
Dennington CEVCP School, Dennington

The Grim Reaper's House

It was a good night for murder
A man as skinny as an elf was
Looking around the house
Bang! went the coffin.
In there was a man, he was alive.

Jack Wood (8)
Dennington CEVCP School, Dennington

The Rotten Candy House

The sticky and smelly rotten marshmallows were
dotted all around the roof.
The raspberry door went *bang!*
The chimney sneezed out lollipops!

Jesse James (8)
Dennington CEVCP School, Dennington

About Pershoe

P ure of heart and fur of silk

E very day he walked and played

R eady with a stick or lick

S uddenly, one day he passed away, he was fifteen.

H e gave cuddles every day.

O nly he could make me smile and turn my frown upside down

E very day he was the dog that made my day.

Mackenzie Banham (11)

Include, Lowestoft

Paddington The Bear

P addington the Bear
A lways there
D efinitely cuter than yours
D efinitely got bigger paws.
I love him.
N ever call him Tim
G rey on the outside
T ough on the inside
O h my goodness, he's so cuddly
N ever take him from me.

Reuben Wade (10)
Include, Lowestoft

Teenagers

T hey are a moaner, groaner and a big d********

E very night they stomp around

E very day they slam around

N ightmare and a piece of work

A lazy sleeper

G roaning all day long

E mbarrassing

R ebellious

S tupid.

Connor Moore (10)

Include, Lowestoft

Messi

Messi is the hat-trick hero
He lived in a tiny home
Messi lived in Argentina
Now he's Barcelona's hero
Rich, famous and lives in a football house
Messi the hat-trick hero.

Andreas Grimble
Include, Lowestoft

We Are Small But Famous

Giant flowers over my head,
People saying, 'Hi!'
I'm just feeling clam and happy
That's who I am now.

Tiny town, tiny town,
That's where I am now,
People singing, dancing,
That's what I can see now.

Someone saying, 'You're up next!'
My heart jumps out right now,
I just started dancing,
And someone shouted, 'You are amazing!'

That's who we are, small but famous.

Karmen Domotor (10)
Laureate Community Academy, Newmarket

Candy Land

Candyland, Candyland,
What a wonderful place to be,
There are candyfloss clouds,
And candy cane trees.

Living in Candyland,
Was a very special fellow,
He was kind and brave,
And went by the name, Marshmallow.

Peace roamed in Candyland until...
One day a big rock candy monster,
Came to terrorise and kill
The poor, poor Candyland civilians.

Then flying in, was little Marshmallow,
Floating in on his laser-shooting deer,
As the monster glared at Marshmallow,
He screamed - like a girl - with fear.

All of a sudden, a flash passed,
The caramel lake bubbled,
The flash made the ground shake and...
The monster fell into the lake.

The civilians laughed and cheered with joy,
Marshmallow was praised by everyone,
A wise old caramel said, 'Well done, little boy.'
And peace was restored in Candyland.

Mehrin Ambia (11)
Laureate Community Academy, Newmarket

The Dragon

I am a dragon, proud and free.
Flying through mountain peaks to my cave I go.
I sit in the mouth of my cave.
I stare up at the starlit sky.
I am a dragon proud and free.
My scales are as black as night.
My wings shine in the moonlight.
I am a dragon proud and free.

Imogen Castang-Wallman (10)
Laureate Community Academy, Newmarket

Fireworks

Bright shiner
Air-glider
Bang-maker
Child-scarer.

Fence-twirler
Sky-lighter
Loud banger
Sparkling sizzler.

Kacey Beau Wing (10)
Laureate Community Academy, Newmarket

When I Saw The Fairies Dancing

When I saw the fairies dancing, there was joy in the air,
When I saw the fairies dancing, they wore bluebell hats,
When I saw the fairies dancing, their little fingers played the flute,
When I saw the fairies dancing, their wings fluttered in laughter,
When I saw the fairies dancing, rabbits held their lanterns.
Their leaf shoes were glistening in the moonlight, damp with dew
And they had a twinkle in their eyes as they sang.
My fingers tingled with excitement whilst I hid behind a bush
With pink blossom dotted around the leaves.
Their cheeks were rosy red and so were their lips,
Sometimes I saw a fairy float up and get a star
And comb their silky hair with it, leaving stardust sprinkled on their head.
The blossom started to make my nose tickle,
I held in the sneeze for as long as I could but sadly the littlest fairy heard me
And whispered something to the others and slowly they all faded away.

The rabbits ran and hid, the stars were back in the sky.
I had just seen the most wonderful thing,
If you see a fairy, close your eyes, run away and don't
tell a soul or a fairy will die.

Georgina Macro (9)
Rattlesden CE Primary Academy, Rattlesden

The Fairies And The Unicorns

There are fairies all around me,
I can't help but shout yippee!
There are fairies all around me,
Then I see them having their tea.

There are fairies all around me,
I see them, they are all dancing,
There are fairies all around me,
Then I see the queen, she's prancing.

There are unicorns all around me,
I can't believe my eyes, they are singing,
There are unicorns all around me,
Then I hear a cheerful bell ringing.

There are unicorns all around me,
Some are running, some are jumping
There are unicorns all around me
Then I hear a terrible thumping.

I open my eyes and I realise it was all just a dream,
My brother is banging on the door,
Giving me a great big smiley beam!

Maizie Carter-Ritchie (9)
Rattlesden CE Primary Academy, Rattlesden

Out In A Forest

O nly we experienced the terrible thing...

U nder our duvets at Jenny's we slept,

T hen all of a sudden, we were surrounded by trees!

I n a split second, we all spun around

N o one believed it, it was a wild boar!

A nother moment flew by; we all got a fright -

F or the boar was charging - straight at us.

O nly Ashton and I weren't hurt, but we paid dearly.

R osie, Jenny, Tracey, Millie and Robert were all hurt.

E ven I had a deep cut in my stomach, but I kept going

S o Ashton and I dragged the others back through a magical portal, appearing just like that.

T hen we all crawled back into bed and slept like logs!

Josephine Bingley (10)

Rattlesden CE Primary Academy, Rattlesden

Parents

You've given me heart,
You've given me soul,
You've given me everything that I know.

You've given me power,
You've given me speed.
You've given me everything that I need.

You've given me nightmares,
You've given me dreams,
You've given me big, bright, light beams.

You've given me liver,
You've given me toes,
You've given me hair I can put up in bows.

I know that you love me so I am never gonna say no!

Harriet Owen-Stiff (11)
Rattlesden CE Primary Academy, Rattlesden

The Girl In The Woods

I found a butterfly in the wood,
I shouldn't follow it,
But I should!

I followed it through the bushes,
I followed it through the trees,
I got nipped by an owl,
And stung by bees!

Through the branches and past the holes
I stepped in one of them
And saw a mole.

I caught the butterfly, *At last*, I thought
I felt warm inside
And that feeling can't be bought.

Katy Gilbrook (9)
Rattlesden CE Primary Academy, Rattlesden

The World Of Dreams

W aking up ruins your dreams

O pening a door to the world of dreams

N ightmares have no place in the world of dreams

D reams are a big part of life

E verything is wonderful in the world of dreams

R ight, left, you lose track of where you are in the world of dreams

F airies, superheroes, anything is possible in the world of dreams

U nusual dreams can occur in the world of dreams

L ovely things can happen in the wonderful world of dreams.

D octors or nurses be what you want in the world of dreams

R ead books in the world of dreams

E verything is awesome in the world of dreams

A nything is possible in the wonderful world of dreams

M onkeys and monsters are real in the world of dreams

S ummer, spring, watch the seasons go past in the world of dreams.

Harriet Glennerster (9)
St Mary's Roman Catholic Primary School, Lowestoft

A Man Of The Shadows. A Man Of The Night

The diamond was stolen deep in the night
Not a being was lurking, all out of sight
The guard was not looking, so he thought he could strike
A man of the shadows, a man of the night.

To many he was known as a mastermind,
Known for his tricks and not walking the line
Mishaps did happen, a life of crime
But not this time... A man of the shadows, a man of the night.

As the alarm bells ring, I wake with a fright
Wow, what an eventful, thrilling excite
I wonder if I will dream of him tonight
... A man of the shadows, a man of the night.

Pippah Olivia Beau Harper-Nunney (10)
St Mary's Roman Catholic Primary School, Lowestoft

There's A Monster In My Cupboard

There's a monster in my cupboard
With dark brown knotted hair
I haven't really seen him
But I'm certain he is there
There's a monster in my cupboard
He's really very tall
I haven't got to measure him
But he makes me feel quite small
There's a monster in my cupboard
From the top down to the floor
But he hides back in the shadows
If I peep around the door
There's a monster in my cupboard
Oh no, I'm very silly.
The monster, he is just a scarf
I wear when I am chilly.

Jessica McDowell (10)
St Mary's Roman Catholic Primary School, Lowestoft

Time Traveller

A time traveller enjoys,
But not always,
Like the dino place,
Or the clown dragons.

But the worst was with Fred,
He went to the wizard monster era,
And got lost for a long time,
Long, long time.

They had superpowers and magic,
He didn't know what to do,
One nearly killed him,
Luckily it didn't.

Finally after years and years,
Guess what, he found the time traveller,
He was so happy,
So he travelled back and was safe.

Matthew Page (9)
St Mary's Roman Catholic Primary School, Lowestoft

Creepy Clowns

Creepy clowns round the corner, creepy clown in the vents,
Creepy clowns in factories, creepy clowns in your head
I was running crack to crack
Looking right behind my back.

I hate these clowns
They're hunting
Me down.
Look at that, it's their hair they call a crown
They're all different colours
Like you and I.

And that laugh
It just sounds so weird
I hope one day they will just disappear.

Inuka Rose (9)
St Mary's Roman Catholic Primary School, Lowestoft

Est.1991

YOUNG WRITERS INFORMATION

We hope you have enjoyed reading this book – and that you will continue to in the coming years.

If you're a young writer who enjoys reading and creative writing, or the parent of an enthusiastic poet or story writer, do visit our website **www.youngwriters.co.uk**. Here you will find free competitions, workshops and games, as well as recommended reads, a poetry glossary and our blog.

If you would like to order further copies of this book, or any of our other titles, then please give us a call or visit **www.youngwriters.co.uk**.

Young Writers
Remus House
Coltsfoot Drive
Peterborough
PE2 9BF
(01733) 890066
info@youngwriters.co.uk